AF226061

Hamilton Troll
and the Case of the
Missing Home

Written By Kathleen J. Shields
Character Illustrations By Leigh A. Klug
Background Illustrations By Carol W. Bryant

Manufactured in the United States of America.

ISBN-13: 978-1-941345-15-3 HardBack
ISBN-13: 978-1-941345-16-0 Paperback
ISBN-Ebook: 9781310547195 Smashwords

Written by Kathleen J. Shields
Inspired by a character Nancy A. Shields envisioned in 1976.
Character Illustrations by Leigh A. Klug
Background Illustrations by Carol W. Bryant

Type font for Hamilton Troll – Berlin Sans FB Demi

To receive notifications of updates or additional
publications, please visit our website:
www.HamiltonTroll.com

It was a wonderful
day that was
almost over
while these two
were walking home.
Chatterton Squirrel
noticed the leaves
that Hamilton
called his
dome.

"I know that your home was flooded one time, so those leaves now cover your hole. They keep it from flooding when the rain pours down and that is your ultimate goal. But why, may I ask, did you dig your home here? When there are so many trees nearby?"

Hamilton smiled
just a bit as he thought
"I will tell you the reason why."

It was a
very cold
December day,
when this gloomy
tale begins.
The leaves had
fallen from the
trees, thanks
to the blowing
winds.

But Hamilton's
tree stood tall
and proud,
evergreen as
it could be.
The smell of pine
was very strong,
from this
amazing tree.

Hamilton sat there alone in his home,
trying to stay warm. When suddenly
the sound of something bad started up
like a thunder storm. It was really quite
noisy, it growled and screamed,
not like the thunder does.
And it kept on growling
without a breath, he didn't
know what
it was.

Afraid to come out
of his hole at that time,
he trembled
in the dark and hid.

As pieces of
pine needles fell in
his hole.
Hamilton
shivered,
he did.

Then all of a sudden as quick as it started,
the awful sound finally stopped. And as
the bright of the day shone in through his
hole, the final pine needle dropped.

He waited a moment or two, maybe three, then stuck his head out his hole. He turned towards his tree and saw it was gone! He nearly lost all control.

He looked at the stump, his eyes opened wide, his heart began beating real quick. He was staring at nothing, in front of his eyes, but it had to have been a bad trick.

He then ran to Merle's, as fast as he could, he sprinted across the ground, and ran through the door with words in his mouth,

"Did you hear that terrible sound?"

Witness - to see something, an event

Merle shook his head no, as he stared at his friend, Hamilton shivered with fright. Merle could see that the trembling troll had witnessed something not right.

Hamilton explained
what he had heard,
while taking Merle's hand.
He dragged his friend out of his home
and raced him across the land.
As they stopped right in front
of Hamilton's home,
Merle did not recognize it.
Without the big tree, so gallant and green,
the scenery just didn't fit.

Gallant - Majestic, thoughtful

Hamilton stared at the stump so in pain,
he couldn't take his eyes off.
But Merle mouse looked off to the distance
and suddenly started to cough.

"Hamilton!" he choked
as he pointed that way,
"Doesn't that look like your tree?"

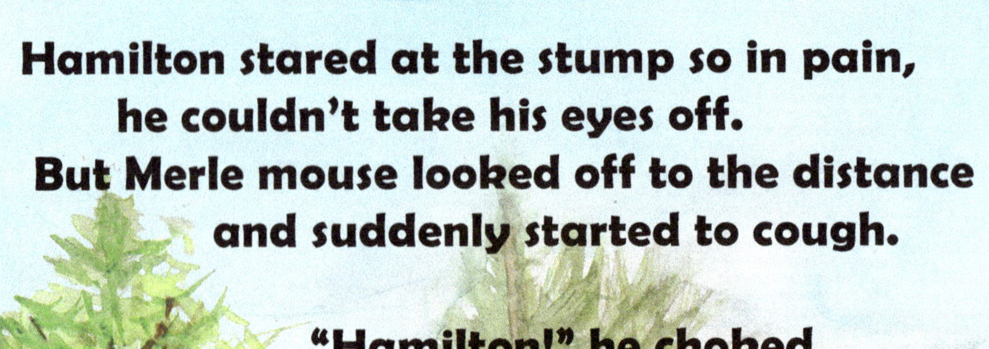

Hamilton looked and watched as they
dragged it, by humans totaling three.

"What are they doing?"
he wondered aloud,
taking in all the details.
A big man and woman
were dragging his tree,
and a child moving
slower than snails.

He watched them walk off
dragging his tree,
he couldn't believe his eyes.
Hamilton just couldn't understand,
he kept asking Merle, "Why?"

"I think this is a case for
Rachel Raccoon, they call her
the creature's detective.
Solving cases and problems,
is all that she does.
Finding answers is Rachel's objective."

Objective - purpose or goal

So they took off towards Rachel's.
They ran really fast.
They didn't stop once at all.
And when they both
struck her door with
all of their force,
they rolled through it
like a very big ball.

"Oh my!"
Rachel spoke
as she stared at the two,
face down out of breath
by her feet.

"I hadn't expected to
have guests stopping by,
but I am glad
you two did,
that is sweet."

Conclusion - decision based on fact, to form an opinion

Rachel had an idea
about this odd case,
a hard conclusion to draw.
She said "I will
        investigate and follow
your tree. The humans
do not bother me.
But Hamilton you must
prepare yourself
to never again
see your tree."

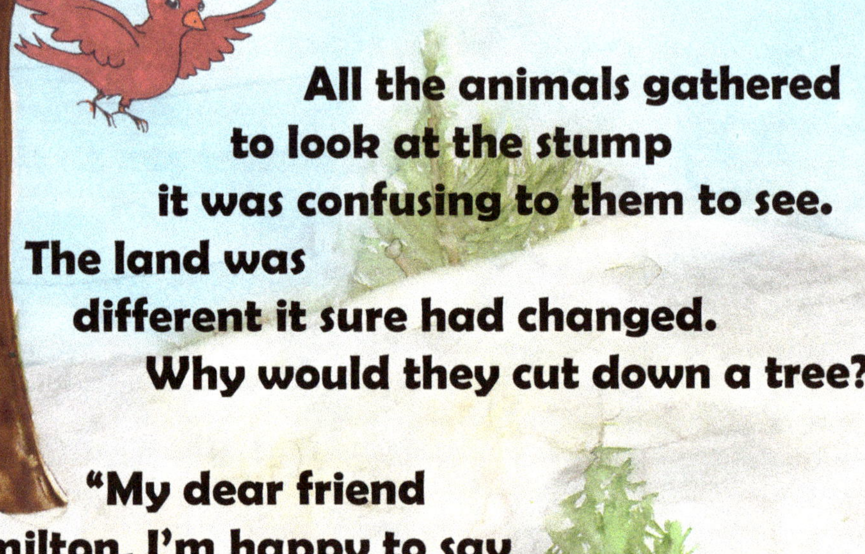

All the animals gathered
to look at the stump
it was confusing to them to see.
The land was
different it sure had changed.
Why would they cut down a tree?

"My dear friend
Hamilton, I'm happy to say
as I look upon
your sad face.
But your tree
has a new home,
a wonderful home.
It really does look in place.

Let me tell you a story
the humans do tell,
it really is quite neat.
It's about beauty
and love and
giving of gifts.
It's a holiday
story time
treat!"

Then she told them the story of
magical Christmas,
colorful, wonderful joy.
Stockings and gifts
and lights with bright colors,
and boxes all filled with toys.

"On Christmas morning
the family will wake
and go sit around
our nice tree.
They'll talk and they'll sing
and share with each other.
It's really a
great sight to see."

Hamilton imagined
what his tree would look like,
and was curious about this day.
He then asked Rachel
if she could take him there,
nothing could keep him away.

So Rachel agreed,
in two morning suns,
we'll go see your
tree on display.
Then you will witness
the wonderful joy
of this
marvelous
magical day.

So Hamilton waited, excited and sad,
his home didn't seem quite the same.
The mornings were brighter
thanks to the sun.
He was grateful
when night time came.

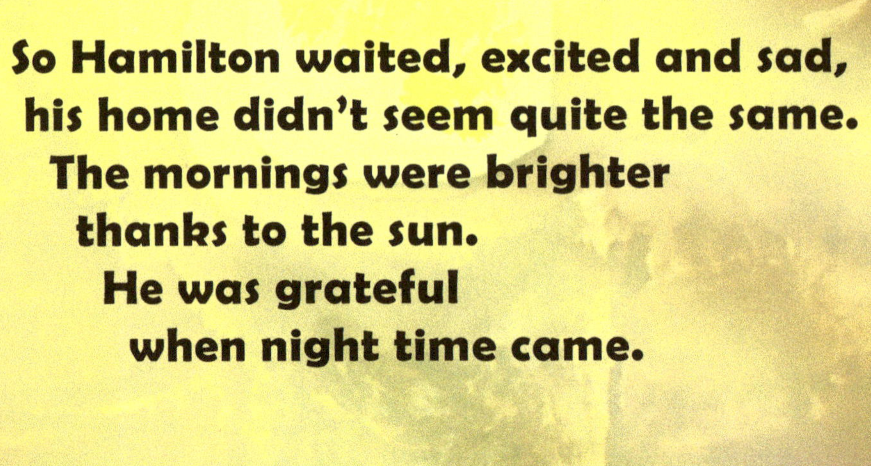

His tree
had provided
shelter and shade.
It had made his home
feel secure.

It would take quite a long time
to get used to this, if he ever would,
he was sure.

So the next early morning
while it was still dark,
he and Rachel
walked into town.

Hamilton was frightened
by the big human things.
He showed his fear with a frown.

As they came to the window
the lights glowing out,
seemed warm with green,
red and gold.

The two of them slowly peeked into the house, the scenery was vibrant and bold.

Vibrant - full of energy, alive

They watched in with silence as the
family came down. Excitement
showed on their face. Then they
settled down together the three,
by the tree and a warm fire place.
Hamilton watched them give gifts, and
smile and stare at his beautiful tree.
It was really a
wonderful
moment to him.
It was truly
worth it to see.

He was proud
of his tree though
he really did miss it.
It gave this family
so much.

It stood proud in their home
beautifully dressed.
To Hamilton
his heart it did touch.

As the two of them left
that morning in silence
the miracle shone
on their face.
Hamilton knew
this was a good thing,
that his tree
wound up
in this place.

"So Chatterton Squirrel," he came to the end, "That explains my lonely tree stump. It may also explain why many loud sounds can easily make me jump.
But most important it speaks of a wonderful day, one that I will always remember. It's a beautiful thing that happens out there, every end of December."

The End

Read Now

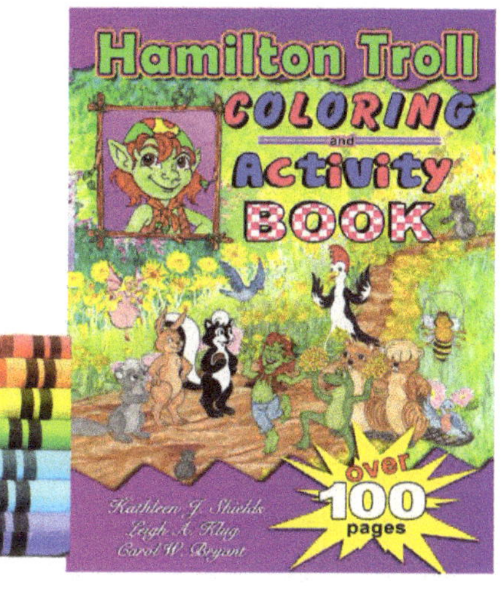

Hamilton Troll
COLORING
and
Activity
BOOK
over 100 pages
Kathleen J. Shields
Leigh A. Klug
Carol W. Bryant

Hamilton Troll
meets
Pink Light Sprite

Hamilton Troll
meets
Skeeter
Skunk

Hamilton Troll
meets
Barney Bee

Hamilton Troll
meets
Chatterton Squirrel

Hamilton Troll
meets
ELWOOD WOODPECKER
Featuring the
BEAVER
BROTHERS

Hamilton Troll
meets
DINOSAURS
2014 First Place TEXAS Picture Book

Hamilton Troll
meets
Whitaker Owl

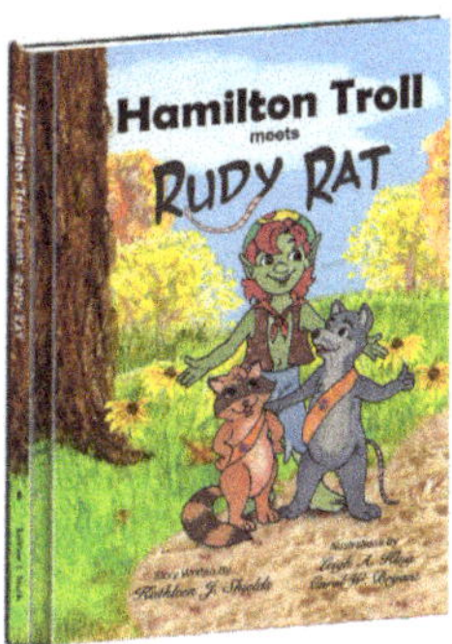

Hamilton Troll
meets
RUDY RAT

Did you find
Pink Light Sprite?

She is hidden in
1 page of this book!

- ➢ Hamilton Troll meets Fiona the Dog
- ➢ Hamilton Troll meets Starlit Troll
- ➢ Hamilton Troll & the Big Race
- ➢ Hamilton Troll Travels the World (New Series)

To receive notifications, updates or play games, please visit our website:

www.HamiltonTroll.com